SPORTS SUPERSTITIONS

GEORGE SULLIVAN

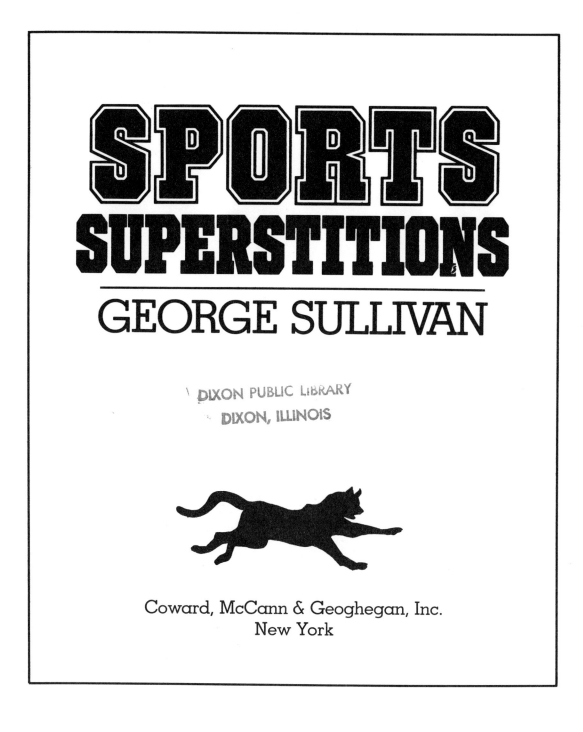

Coward, McCann & Geoghegan, Inc.
New York

All photos courtesy of George Sullivan, with the exception of the following: p. 6—Photography, Inc., Inglewood, Calif.; p. 7—John Devaney, New York, N.Y.; p. 13—CBS-TV Sports; p. 23—Wake Forest University; p. 34—Rod Hanna, Topeka Capital-Journal; p. 49—Wagner International, New York, N.Y.; p. 58—Budd, New York, N.Y.; p. 61—Yonkers Raceway, Michael Cipriani; p. 70—Pennsylvania State University.

Library of Congress Cataloging in Publication Data

Sullivan, George.   Sports superstitions.
SUMMARY: A survey of superstitions in the world of sports including those of superstars such as Phil Esposito, Nadia Comaneci, and Joe Namath.
    Includes index.
1. Sports (in religion, folklore, etc.) 2. Superstition.
1. Sports (in religion, folklore, etc.) 2. Superstition
I. Title.
GR887.S9   398′.41   78-62   ISBN 0-698-20439-5

Introduction

*D*o you fear black cats, witches, or consider 13 to be an unlucky number? Do you avoid walking under ladders or believe that a broken mirror means bad luck? Do you wear a charm to ward off misfortune, or have you ever used a lucky pen to take an examination?

If you answered "yes" to any of these questions, you're superstitious.

It's not likely, however, that your superstitious beliefs are as serious as those of the average athlete. Lady Luck never misses a sports event—or so most participants believe.

Some baseball players would rather walk barefoot over broken glass than step on a chalked foul line. Most football coaches will not permit their players to be quartered on a hotel's thirteenth floor. There are countless auto-racing mechanics who still shrink in horror at the sight of a woman in the garage area.

Another common sports superstition involves clothing. The same socks and shoes, or pants and jerseys, are donned day after day to preserve a run of good luck.

Most superstitious beliefs and practices date to ancient times. Primitive people often lived in terror of the forces of nature and feared the spirits that they believed dwelled in trees, rocks, springs, caves, and on mountaintops.

Different beliefs developed for warding off evil, preventing sickness, or foretelling the future.

Scientific thought has helped to destroy some superstitions by telling us that everything in nature has a natural cause. Nevertheless, in our daily life, superstitious habits still persist. In the world of sports, they flourish!

3

*P*hil Esposito, who joined the New York Rangers in 1976 after a glittering career with the Boston Bruins, was perhaps the most superstitious of all hockey players. Esposito had no idea, of course, how much his bizarre practices had to do with the fact that he set several National Hockey League scoring records, but they were as important to him as well-sharpened skates, and year by year he added to the rites he performed.

In the locker room before a game, Esposito would carefully lay out all of his equipment. He would place his stick on the bench, lining it up so that it was perfectly parallel to the bench itself. Then he would place the left-hand glove to the right of the stick and the right-hand glove to the stick's left. The heels of the gloves were lined up with the butt end of the stick.

Esposito always wore an old black T-shirt inside out. He traced the practice to a night when he arrived for a game with a stiff neck. He put on the black shirt to keep in his body heat. The stiff neck disappeared. More important, he scored three goals that night. That made Esposito a black-shirt believer for all time.

Esposito's hockey stick got special treatment. He always wrapped it with black friction tape, and he would not take it out of the dressing room until the team's trainer had sprinkled it with talcum powder.

Crossed sticks in the locker room were always a sign of bad luck to Esposito. Occasionally a locker-room prankster would place crossed sticks in front of Esposito's dressing stall. Then he'd hide, waiting for the explosion that was sure to follow.

5

Esposito's fans were aware of his superstitious nature and used to send him good-luck trinkets. Many of these took the form of small animal horns, a charm well known for its "protective" powers. You can't purchase such a charm and expect it to be effective. It must be given to you by a friend, so custom dictates.

Esposito hung these and other charms in his locker. Toward the end of his career, his locker became so cluttered with them that he had trouble finding space to hang his clothes.

In auto racing, the superstition used to prevail that it was unlucky for a woman to be seen in the garage area of a track. Mechanics so feared the sight of a woman that rules were adopted at many race courses forbidding them to enter the garage area.

Women reporters and photographers were even barred from the garage area of the Indianapolis 500, the most noted of all racing events. They were until 1971, that is. That year two female reporters obtained a court order permitting them to enter the garage area at Indy. The ban was never reinstated.

While this superstition is said to be dying out, it lingers on at some of the country's smaller race courses. Sports photographer Ellen Griesedieck once recalled being assigned to take photographs at a track in 1973. "I had to do it undercover," she said. "I had to dress up in overalls, stuff my hair under a cap, and wear sunglasses in order to get into the garage area."

At the end of the day when her work was finished, she went up to the official who had barred her entrance, pulled off her hat and glasses, and said, "Well, thanks a lot. It was great."

"He couldn't believe it," she recalled. "He just stood there staring."

The electrifying Pelé, a member of the New York Cosmos of the North American Soccer League from 1975 to 1977, is probably the best-known athlete in the world. He won international fame for his amazing exploits as a member of Brazil's Santos team, and for leading his native country to victory in soccer's World Cup competition in 1958, 1962, and 1970.

Pelé believed that the number 10, which he always wore, had special significance for him. In World Cup play, players don't wear their regular numbers; they must draw for new ones. Pelé, in the first of his World Cup appearances in 1958, drew the number 10. Then in 1962, Pelé drew again, and again he pulled the number 10.

There are 18 players on World Cup squads. The odds of getting a particular number once are 18 to 1. The odds of doing it a second time are an incredible 324 to 1.

Before the World Cup competition in 1966, Brazilian officials decided that Pelé wouldn't have to draw the number 10. They gave it to him permanently. When Pelé joined the Cosmos, the club issued him number 10 right away.

His uniform number wasn't the only place that Pelé encountered the number 10. "When Pelé gets a hotel room, he is often assigned the room 1010," according to Giora Breil, his business manager. "The digits of my office number—2008—add up to 10," he pointed out. "And Pelé's real name—Nascimento—has ten letters."

Christopher (Christy) Mathewson, a pitching great for the New York Giants in the early 1900s, called baseball "the child of superstition." Said Mathewson: "A jinx can make a bad pitcher out of a good one, and a blind batter out of a .300 hitter."

It's just as true today as it was in Mathewson's time. In the clubhouse, in the dugout, and on the field, superstitious practices abound. In fact, baseball players are probably more superstitious than athletes in any other sport.

Why should this be true? One reason is because baseball is a game that stresses individual effort. There's not the feeling of team play that one gets in football, soccer, and ice hockey.

Since baseball is a personal game, one's mental attitude is all-important. A superstitious belief can help a player take his mind off whatever fears he might have. It can bolster his confidence.

There's another reason, too. Baseball, as compared to most other sports, is played in rather a leisurely fashion. There's plenty of time in which to develop a ritual; there's time to be able to indulge in it.

Los Angeles Dodgers first baseman Steve Garvey, the National League's Most Valuable Player in 1974, has had many superstitions. His favorite helped his hitting, he believed. "If I'm going well at the plate," he has said, "I'll take exactly the same number of practice swings each time at bat."

Jim Palmer, the ace right-hander of the Baltimore Orioles, has always sat on the exact same spot in the dugout through the first five or six innings of play. He would not change unless the Orioles failed to score. Then he'd look for another seat.

Pitcher Mike Cuellar, once a teammate of Palmer's, believed it was bad luck for anyone but a catcher to warm him up between innings. On most teams, an infielder will grab a mitt and take the pitcher's warm-up pitches while the regular catcher gets into his gear. But no infielder on the Orioles ever did that. Cuellar would always stand on the mound and wait for the catcher.

Manny Sanguillen of the Oakland A's has always scuffed out the back line of the batter's box when stepping in. Pitcher Doug Rau of the Dodgers has never

11

touched a baseball with his pitching hand the day before he pitched. He would wear a batting glove on his throwing hand so he'd be forced to use the other hand.

The Mets' Bud Harrelson has never walked in front of the umpire and catcher when walking up to the plate. But Jackie Robinson of the Brooklyn Dodgers always walked in front of the catcher to reach the batter's box. If the catcher happened to be out at the mound talking to the pitcher, Robinson would wait in the on-deck circle for him to come back.

The Cardinals' hard-hitting Ted Simmons has not permitted anybody to use his bat when he is on a hot streak at the plate. Carlton Fisk of the Red Sox has not allowed himself to get caught in the clubhouse when the national anthem is being played. "One time," he recalled, "I had to go into the locker room to change my sweat shirt, when the first notes sounded. We lost that day and I had a miserable game. I've been on the field ever since."

Even the coaches get involved. Denny Sanders, third-base coach for the New York Mets, has trotted from home plate to third base when taking up his post each inning, striding on the foul line as he ran. Jerry Adair, first-base coach for the Orioles, always started the infield warm-up by bringing the ball from the dugout and tossing it to the first baseman. None of the Oriole infielders would think of starting the warm-up session. They all waited for Adair.

Some players talk openly about their superstitions. Others won't, saying only that they follow certain "habits" or "routines." But the truth is that the hex, the jinx, the good omen, and the bad are almost as much a part of baseball as strikeouts and home runs.

adia Comaneci, who thrilled spectators at the 1976 Olympic Games, winning five gold medals and becoming the youngest gymnastics champion in Olympic history, has permitted herself one superstitious practice. In 1968, when she was seven years old, her coach, Bela Karolyi, entered Nadia in the Romanian National Junior Gymnastics Championships. Nadia finished in thirteenth place.

Afterward, Karolyi bought Nadia an Eskimo doll with a sealskin dress as a good-luck charm. He told Nadia that she must never finish thirteenth again.

The next year Nadia took the doll with her when she competed in the junior championships a second time. And this time she won. From then on, whenever Nadia traveled to gymnastics meets, she carried the doll with her. And it accompanied her to Montreal in the summer of 1976, when she dazzled the world with her magical performances.

Bowler Patty Costello had averaged a stunning 226 for forty-eight games but still needed two strikes in a row—a double—in the tenth and final frame of the 1976 U.S. Open in Tulsa, Oklahoma, to beat Betty Morris.

If she was nervous, she didn't show it. The twenty-nine-year-old left-hander from Scranton, Pennsylvania, looked like there wasn't the slightest doubt in her mind she would get the two consecutive strikes.

It could have been the color of the blouse and skirt she was wearing—yellow. "I always wear yellow when I want to build my confidence," Patty has said. "It makes me feel like I can't lose."

Patty got the double, won the game with a 235 score, and captured the Open, earning $6,000. It was her seventh tournament victory of 1976, a performance that earned her a second Bowler of the Year award. She had first been named Bowler of the Year in 1972, a year she had won 5 tournaments.

Patty has never bowled without wearing two lucky rings on her right hand. The one she's worn on her index finger has a twin diamond setting. The other, worn on her little finger, is an opal, a milky-white stone that changes color with the light.

"The rings are important to me," Patty said, "and I wouldn't dream of bowling without wearing them.

"But my big thing is the clothes I wear, their color.

"Say I'm in the final games of an important tournament. I've been bowling for several days, and I'm a little bit weary. Then I'll wear red, a red blouse and a red skirt. Red charges me up. I've bowled some of the highest games of my career wearing red."

Green has been another of Patty's lucky colors. "Green is my money color," she's said. "A green blouse and a green-print skirt make me think of how much prize money I can win if I bowl well. I often wear green in the final games of a tournament."

Patty has worn blue when she wanted to relax. She's worn yellow, her confidence-builder, any time she's had a good chance of winning.

She considers black unlucky. "I once wore black in a tournament and bowled badly," she said. "I'd never wear black again."

Patty's 212 average during 1976 was the best among women and higher than some male professionals. "I'd love to compete on the men's tour," she has said. "I feel sure I could make the finals often, and have a good chance to win at least one tournament a year."

Of course, the men would have to let Patty wear the colors of her choice.

Man Mountain Harvey Martin, the Dallas Cowboys' huge defensive end, has become frantic if he could not eat at least two hot dogs before a game. If the Dallas trainer or a locker-room attendant were unable to provide Martin with his required pre-game fare, he would rush to a concession counter or seek out a vendor in the stands. Since he often was fully uniformed when chasing through the stands, he made an unusual sight. But comments about Martin's bizarre conduct were few; after all, he stands 6 feet 5 inches and weighs 262 pounds.

Defensive tackle Dewey Selmon of the Tampa Bay Buccaneers has always put a dime beneath the inner sole of his shoe before a game. "I put the dime in there for the first time before the game with Texas during my sophomore year [1973] at Oklahoma," Dewey recalled. "When we won the game, 54–13, I decided to keep putting the dime in my shoe.

"Once I forgot, and it bothered me for the whole first period. I finally asked one of the coaches on the sidelines to let me borrow a dime."

When Frank Lucchesi managed the Texas Rangers from 1975 to 1977, he was known as "Hippity Hop" because of his fear of stepping on the foul lines. Lucchesi would almost do back-flips to avoid them.

Not stepping on the foul lines or bases in going to and from one's position is perhaps baseball's most common superstition. Many players follow it.

The Cardinals' Lou Brock, who became baseball's all-time base-stealing king in 1977, admitted that he has never stepped on second base on his way to his position in the outfield. "I did it a few times," he once said, "and it never failed—the other team scored in that inning. I just won't do it anymore."

Mel Stottlemyre, the splendid Yankee right-handed pitcher who retired in 1974, was another player who never stepped on the foul line. He once explained why: "We were playing the Twins, and I was headed for the bullpen to warm up before the start of the game. I avoided the foul line and Jim Hegan, a Yankee coach, said I shouldn't be superstitious, that I should step on the line. So I did.

"The first batter I faced was Ted Uhlaender, and he hit a line drive off my left shin. It went for a hit. Then Rod Carew, Tony Oliva, and Harmon Killebrew followed with base hits. The fifth man hit a single and scored. I was charged with five runs.

"I never stepped on a foul line again."

It seems odd, but while many players seek to avoid the foul lines and bases, others make it a point *to* step on them. Joe Rudi of the California Angels has always stepped on third base on his way to the dugout. Pitcher John (Blue Moon) Odom always touched the foul line on the way to the mound in his many seasons with the Oakland A's.

Luis Aparicio, the slick fielding shortstop for the Boston Red Sox, followed the same practice, always stepping on third base on the way to his position. The Minnesota Twins were aware of Aparicio's habit. Once, when the infield was being smoothed out at the top of the fifth inning, the Minnesota players convinced the ground crew not to put down third base right away.

When Aparicio ran out of the dugout, he saw first and second base in place, but there was no third. He couldn't believe his eyes. Not until he heard laughter coming from the Twins' dugout did he realize what was going on.

While foul lines and bases didn't bother the controversial Mike Marshall, who pitched for half a dozen different teams in his ten-year career, Marshall had a mania of his own. He *always* walked to the mound from the first-base side of the field, even when his team's dugout was on the third-base line. The Yankees' Lefty Gomez also used to follow the same practice.

John (Pepper) Martin and Joe (Ducky) Medwick, two members of the St. Louis Cardinals' colorful "Gashouse Gang" of the 1930s, were both superstitious. One of their beliefs was that it was good luck to find a hairpin.

Once, when Martin was in a batting slump, Cardinal manager Frankie Frisch bought some hairpins and scattered them in front of the St. Louis dugout. Frisch figured that when Martin discovered the pins, he'd believe his luck had changed, and he'd start hitting the ball again.

However, Ducky Medwick came out of the dugout first. When he saw the hairpins, he let out a joyous cry and started picking them up.

"Hey!" yelled Frisch. "What are you doing? Those pins are for Martin. Let them alone."

"To heck with Martin," Medwick shouted back. "Let him find his own pins!"

Several weeks before the New York Giants opened their 1976 football season, four members of the team—defensive end Jack Gregory, guard Tom Mullen, linebacker Brian Kelley, and fullback Larry Csonka—rented a stately old house on the shores of the Hudson River in Piermont, New York, and planned to live there together until the season ended and they could return to their homes. Piermont was an easy drive to both the Giants' new stadium in East Rutherford, New Jersey, and the club's training camp at Pleasantville, New York.

"We had some differences at first," Kelley once recalled, "but generally we got along well and saw eye-to-eye on most things." But it was not their relationships that were to cause the players difficulty. It was the house itself. Before the season ended, it was to be branded as the "Giants' jinx house."

Misfortune struck Jack Gregory first. Late in the season, as the Giants were losing to the Denver Broncos, Gregory suffered torn ligaments in his left knee. While he was spared surgery, he was placed on the disabled list and sent home for the rest of the season.

Larry Csonka was next. In seven seasons with the Miami Dolphins and in the one season he had spent with Memphis in the World Football League, a period in which he had won acclaim as pro football's Number 1 running back, Csonka had never suffered a serious leg injury.

The Giants were battling the Seattle Seahawks at their New Jersey home on the last Sunday in November. Csonka took a handoff, tucked the ball to his belly, and ripped through the Seattle line for an 11-yard gain. A wave of tacklers hit him head on. When Csonka fell backward, his left knee got twisted in one direction, the foot in another. Csonka screamed in pain and grabbed the knee with both hands.

Doctors soon confirmed what Csonka suspected. He had torn ligaments in the left knee and would require surgery. His season was over, his career jeopardized.

Csonka's injury occurred in the second quarter of the game against the Seahawks. Tom Mullen was the victim in the third quarter. Attempting to defend quarterback Craig Morton, who had dropped back to pass, Mullen got caught in a crowd and, as he was going down, felt something "pop" in his knee.

Late that night, Mullen, with a huge bandage around his right knee, returned to the house in Piermont and packed his belongings. Then Kelley drove him to the hospital in New York where surgery was to be performed the next day.

"Three down and one left," Kelley thought to himself as he drove back to Piermont late that night. The very next morning he moved into a motel.

"It's not superstition or anything like that," he was to say later. "But just to be on the safe side. . . ."

Among professional golfers, Tom Weiskopf has followed a set of dos and don'ts that will never be found in any instruction book. "I never go out on a course without three pennies in my pocket," said Weiskopf. "Also, three tees. And I won't tee off on a par-three hole except with a broken tee which I pick up."

Even Jack Nicklaus, the greatest golfer of the 1970s, has admitted that he, too, liked to have three pennies in his pocket when starting a round. "I just don't feel secure otherwise," he's said.

Byron Nelson sat on a stool in the clubhouse of the Augusta National Country Club, preparing to go out onto the course for the final round of the 1937 U.S. Masters Championship. He was right on the heels of Ralph Guldahl, the leader.

Nelson reached into his locker and took out a box containing a dozen brand-new golf balls. He broke open the cover and ripped away the cellophane from the four little packages inside. Each package contained three balls, all seemingly exactly alike. But they weren't alike to Nelson. He rejected one ball from each box of three, then handed the others to his caddy.

Before he went out onto the course, Nelson was asked why he had discarded some balls. "They're all good balls and I guess one will go as far and as straight as another, if you hit it right," he said. "But you'll notice in each package one ball is marked with blue letters, one with green, and one with red.

"Well, I don't like to play with the ones that have red markings, that's all."

"Is that a superstition?" Nelson was asked.

Nelson didn't answer. He just shrugged and grinned.

P.S. Nelson won the Masters title that year.

*T*ennis is like baseball in that it is a game in which individual effort is stressed. Many of the individuals who play the game develop an array of superstitious habits.

Greer (Cat) Stevens of the Boston Lobsters, one of the hard-hitting young stars of World Team Tennis, has always considered it good luck to hit her forehand strokes with the front side of her racket, and her backhand strokes with the other side. (The manufacturer's name and trademark distinguish the front side of the racket from the back.)

As she awaited an opponent's serve, Cat would twirl the racket nervously, the way a batter might swish his bat back and forth as the pitcher winds up. But she always made sure the racket ended up with the front side ready to receive strokes from the forehand side.

Named the Rookie of the Year in World Team Tennis in 1975, Cat has another superstition that is a tradition in her family. She never laces up the two top eyelets of her tennis shoes. "I got that from my mom," she says. "She never laced up her shoes to the top, either."

Countless players develop superstitious feelings about the balls. Dick Stockton, America's seventh-ranked player in 1976, was one. "If I lose a point," said Stockton, "I punish the ball by refusing to play the next point with it."

The opposite also applies. When a player wins a point, he makes sure that he uses the same ball for the ensuing point.

The gifted Vijay Amritraj, who was born in Madras, India, has always been careful about how he got out of bed in the morning. If he happened to get out on the right side and he won his match that day, he'd make sure he got out on the right side the next morning. "I'd do it," said Amritraj, "even if I had to crawl out of the end."

South Africa's John Yuill, when changing courts with an opponent, has always crossed diagonally, timing his steps so that his left foot swung over the intersection of the sideline and the service line.

Many tennis habits involve serving, and are apparent in those tense moments just before the player tosses the ball up to hit it. Raul Ramirez has rolled the ball on his shirt before serving. Ceci Martinez has touched it to her forehead.

Rod Laver has blown on his hand before he served. Jimmy Connors and Billy Martin later adopted this practice.

Connors has displayed many nervous mannerisms. As the pressure of the match built, Connors has tugged his shirt sleeve, examined his fingertips, and adjusted the positioning of his racket strings.

On his way to victory at Wimbledon in 1974, Connors seemed preoccupied with the number 4. He did everything in fours. Before serving, he never failed to bounce the ball four times. He tapped things four times. Once, when the players were changing sides, Connors took a sip from his cup of soda, then tapped it three times on the cooler. He started out onto the court, then suddenly remembered that he had tapped the cup only three times, and he went back and tapped it one more time.

𝓑ill Bradley of the New York Knickerbockers, from 1967 to 1976 a favorite of throngs that packed Madison Square Garden, used to go through a nightly ritual that was seldom noticed by any of the fans.

At every time-out, the players would form a semicircle around coach Red Holzman. The team's trainer, Danny Whelan, would pass out towels to the players. Each man would wipe off the perspiration and then toss the towel toward the bench or hand it back to Whelan—except for Bradley. He would place his towel on Whelan's right shoulder, folding it neatly. He did this perhaps a dozen times a game, and over the season, about a thousand times. "I can't really say that it helped my jump shot," said Bradley, "but I'm sure it had some effect, whether it's just in my mind or not."

What happens when a team wins a championship? The players celebrate with champagne. It's a tradition that's as firmly fixed as night baseball.

Red Auerbach, both as a coach and general manager of the Boston Celtics, pro basketball's winningest team of all time, has had a superstition about champagne in the locker room. Most teams on the brink of a championship purchase their champagne and store it until the festive moment. Not the Celtics. Auerbach didn't even want to hear the word "champagne" until the title was nailed down.

This caused the Celtics problems in 1974, the year they faced the Milwaukee Bucks in the play-off finals. Auerbach would not allow champagne into the locker room before the seventh and deciding game. In fact, he would not even permit club officials to buy champagne.

Of course, you know what happened—the Celtics won. In order to do their celebrating, they had to borrow champagne from the defeated Milwaukee team.

The Baltimore Colts were the surprise team of the 1975 pro football season. They were not even expected to be title contenders. But after losing four of their first five games, the Colts went on a rampage, defeating one opponent after another.

Most people gave the lion's share of the credit to quarterback Bert Jones, who emerged as football's Number 1 passer and signal-caller that season. Coach Ted Marchibroda had another reason. His yellow shirt.

Marchibroda wore the shirt on October 26 when the Colts beat the Jets. He wore it the next week, and his team whipped the Cleveland Browns. You can guess what happened in the weeks that followed. Marchibroda kept wearing the shirt, and the Colts kept winning. In fact, they won nine straight games, a streak that carried them to the championship of their division.

The newspapers in Baltimore called it "The Miracle of 33rd Street." (Balti-

27

more's Memorial Stadium, where the Colts played their home games, is located on 33rd Street.) Marchibroda would be the first to admit that indeed there was something miraculous involved.

Marchibroda's experience is one example of a common sports superstition, that of wearing lucky clothing. Football coaches have been known to stick to their lucky hats, suits, socks, or shoes to keep winning. Baseball players often wear the same parts of their uniform day after day to keep a hot streak going.

Yankee outfielder Roy White has made it a point to wear the same shoes and sweat shirt if he was hitting the ball well. Pitcher Jim Palmer of the Baltimore Orioles, the American League's Cy Young Award winner for 1976, believed in the good luck of wearing the same pair of socks all season long.

It's not just baseball and football—every sport seems affected by this superstition. Golfer Johnny Farrell, who won the U.S. Open Championship in 1928 at the Olympic Fields Course in Matteson, Illinois, sincerely believed that a green sweater he wore was a big help.

Farrell wore the sweater on each day of the early rounds. The tournament ended in a tie between Farrell and Bobby Jones. A play-off round was necessary to break the tie.

Farrell was careful to don the sweater as the play-off round began. The day was sweltering. After a few holes, Farrell could not stand the heat any longer. He removed the sweater and tucked it in the pocket of his golf bag.

Immediately he started slipping. He decided he'd better put the sweater back on. His championship touch returned.

With two holes to play, Farrell had a one-stroke lead. Jones, in a driving finish, poured in birdies on those last two holes. But Farrell matched him stroke for stroke, also getting two birdies to maintain his lead. Afterward, Farrell said that he doubted whether he could have done it without the green sweater.

Gene Tunney, the world's former heavyweight boxing champion, pinned his faith on an old and battered bathrobe that he had worn the night he won the Marine Corps light heavyweight championship during World War I.

Not long before he met Jack Dempsey for the heavyweight title in Philadelphia in 1926, Tunney's friends presented him with a handsome blue satin robe bearing the Marine Corps emblem in gold. When Tunney entered the ring to face Dempsey, he wore the new robe—but he had on the old frayed relic underneath.

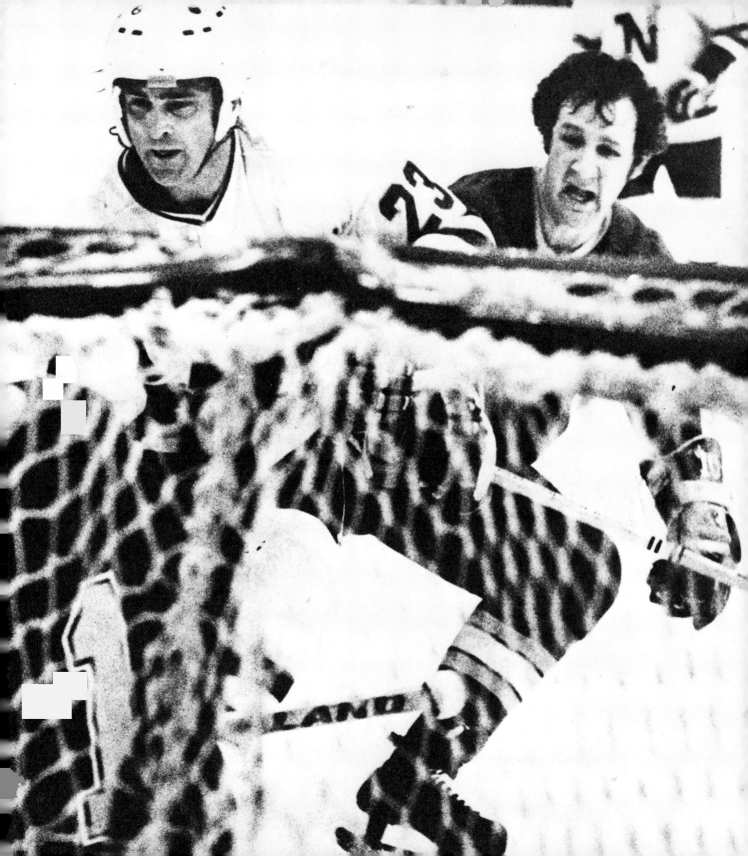

ou Nanne, who played an assortment of positions with the Minnesota North Stars in his decade as a hockey player, had an unusual routine he followed whenever a period ended. He'd immediately go into the washroom and blow his nose twice. Always twice.

"After that," he once recalled, "I'd walk back to my locker, sit down, and unlace five eyelets on each of my skates." It had to be *five* eyelets. During his early years with the North Stars, Nanne unlaced only three eyelets on each boot. Year by year the number of goals he scored kept getting larger, hitting a high of 21 in the 1971–1972 season. But the next season Nanne's total tumbled to 15.

"That's when I switched to five eyelets," says Nanne. "It made me feel luckier to do five."

Tennis star Martina Navratilova created headlines around the world in 1975 when she announced she was leaving her native Czechoslovakia for permanent residence in the United States. She won her first Wimbledon title the next year, teaming with Chris Evert to capture the doubles crown over Billie Jean King and Betty Stove. Martina was nineteen at the time.

Martina has admitted to being "very superstitious." She has worn the same pair of shoes for an entire tournament. She has often decided upon a favorite "side" in an arena and chosen it when she won the toss at the beginning of a match.

She has not stepped out onto the court without donning certain pieces of jewelry. What she has worn includes a gold bracelet and a diamond-studded wristwatch, both on her right wrist, since she's a left-hander.

She's also worn special trinkets on thin gold chains around her neck. One is a heart-shaped piece of jewelry encrusted with small diamonds. "It's a gift from a friend," she's said. From another chain hangs one of a pair of dice. "I wear that because I love backgammon," Martina said. (In the game of backgammon, moves are determined by throws of the dice.)

From still another chain hangs a small rectangular tag that resembles a price tag. It's made of gold. One word has been engraved upon it: "Expensive."

Martina has always traveled with a dog, a small black poodle named "Racket." "He brings me good luck, too," Martina said.

Through the centuries, lucky charms have taken all kinds of forms. In eighteenth-century England, it was believed that you could cure certain aches and pains by carrying a raw potato in your pocket. The knuckle bone of a sheep worn about the neck was thought to have the same power.

Elephant hair carried in a locket has been hailed for the good luck it brings. There's the four-leaf clover, of course, and the most popular charm of all, the rabbit's foot. (It must be the left hind foot of the rabbit, however.)

No one knows for sure exactly how the rabbit's foot superstition began.

One source says that it is derived from the fact that young rabbits are born with their eyes open. The animal was thus believed to have power over the evil eye.

Another source says that rabbits have become associated with prosperity and success because of their ability to produce offspring in large numbers. Whatever the reason, the rabbit's foot has always served as a convenient token of the animal's power.

The rabbit's foot once affected the outcome of a baseball game. It happened on June 4, 1951. The Cleveland Indians faced the New York Yankees at Cleveland Stadium.

Ed Lopat was to pitch for the Yankees. A canny curveball specialist, Lopat was in the midst of an impressive career. He was never more impressive than when he faced the Indians. He had beaten Cleveland thirty times in thirty-six decisions, and now boasted an eleven-game winning streak against the team.

So desperate had the situation become for local fans that a Cleveland newspaper asked for suggestions as to how the Indians might tame Lopat. One fan suggested giving a rabbit's foot to everyone attending Lopat's next game in Cleveland. The Indian management agreed to go along. On the night Lopat was scheduled to pitch, 15,000 rabbits' feet were distributed among 20,217 fans.

After Lopat had finished his warm-up throws, a rabbit was brought to the mound and presented to him. Lopat smiled agreeably.

He managed to get the first man out. Then came a single, double, and two more singles in that order by Ray Boone, Larry Doby, Luke Easter, and Al Rosen. Two runs scored.

After Ray Chapman flied out, Bob Kennedy homered. That made it 5–0. The crowd loved it.

After Lopat gave up another run in the second inning, manager Casey Stengel called in a relief hurler. As Lopat made his way to the dugout, his chin on his chest, the Cleveland fans screamed in delight. Many of them waved their rabbits' feet or simply held them aloft in triumph. The Cleveland team went on to win, 8–2.

The rabbit's foot was established as a prime source of good luck in the minds of thousands of Clevelanders that night. In Eddie Lopat's mind, however, the charm took on a much different meaning.

While many baseball players have undue concern about the foul lines, with professional football players it's taping. Teams make it mandatory that each player have his ankles taped before each game and most practice sessions. It's a precaution meant to cut down on ankle injuries.

Most players insist that either the right foot or left foot always be taped first. Other players will permit only one man to do the taping. Ed O'Bradovich of the Chicago Bears once had his ankles taped by equipment manager Bill Martel, and Ed had a good game. From that day on, O'Bradovich would never allow anyone but Martel to tape him. Even if Martel happened to be busy distributing uniforms before a game, it wouldn't matter to O'Bradovich. He made him stop to apply his tape.

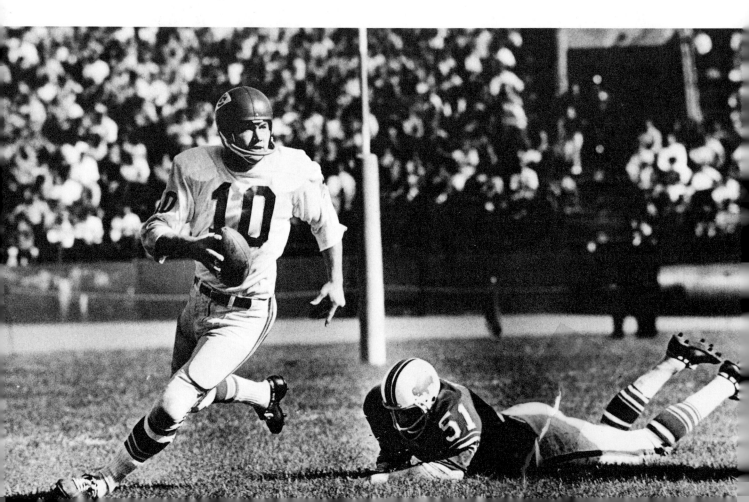

*T*rack stars Cheryl Toussaint, winner of a silver medal in the 1972 Olympic Games, and Lorna Forde, who ran for Barbados in the 1972 and 1976 Olympics but later moved to New York City, both indulged in a superstition that is widespread in track and field.

They never let anyone "cross their legs."

Suppose you, as a track competitor, are sitting on the ground, legs stretched out in front of you, waiting for your scheduled events to be called. Another runner approaches and attempts to step over your legs—"cross" them. You must not permit it. It's certain bad luck.

Fred Thompson, founder and coach of the New York Atoms Track Club of New York, one of the strongest clubs in the country, has called this the most popular of all track superstitions. "It gets passed down from athlete to athlete," he said.

35

If a person should catch you unaware and succeed in crossing your legs, you must make the person cross back. It's the only way to remove the bad luck.

Almost as popular is the custom of "not splitting a pole." If two competitors are walking together and come to an upright post, tradition demands that both must pass the pole on the same side. They can't let the pole divide —or "split"—them.

To many athletes, these two superstitions are almost as important as getting fast starts and taking long strides. "Everybody knows about them," said Fred Thompson.

For decades, automobile race drivers feared the color green. The superstition was supposed to have breathed its last in 1965, the year that Jim Clark won the Indianapolis 500 in a green Lotus-Ford. The color green had no special meaning to Clark.

But the superstition never really died. Mario Andretti, one of America's most noted race drivers of recent times, admitted the color green has always bothered him. "I'm not a superstitious man," said Andretti, "but I never sign an autograph when someone hands me a green pen. The people don't understand, but I can't help that."

Mountaineering, that is, climbing mountains as a sport, is a popular pastime. There are an estimated half-million mountain climbers in the world today.

But at one time, mountaineering was drenched in superstition. To climb a tall mountain used to be regarded as being about as foolhardy as trying to swim the Atlantic Ocean. You didn't do it with any thought of survival.

Mountains, with their forbidding heights, shrouded in swirling clouds, were looked upon with awe. They were believed to be the place where spirits lurked. The feeling was universal, and applied as much to Fuji, the tallest mountain in Japan, as it did to lofty Olympus in Greece, or Mt. Everest in the Himalayas, the highest peak in the world.

In the Old Testament, Lot expressed a typical attitude toward mountains. Reluctant to leave the cities of the plains, he says, "I cannot escape to the mountain, lest evil overtake me and I die" (Genesis 19:19).

In the Bible, mountain summits were often considered to be within God's personal domain. Men ascended mountains to communicate directly with the divine. Mt. Sinai was where Moses went to receive the law of God. It was from Mt. Nebo that he was permitted to see the Promised Land. And it was from Mt. Carmel that Elijah's servant saw the cloud—"as small as a man's hand"—approach from the Mediterranean, bringing the promise of rain and an end to a terrible drought.

Little wonder, then, that mountain peaks continued to be regarded as forbidden places for centuries. One of the first recorded attempts at an ascent was made in 1387. Six clergymen decided to climb Mt. Pilatus in the Swiss Alps. They wanted to destroy the superstitious belief that the spirit of Pontius Pilate, who had ordered the crucifixion of Christ, lived in a marshy lake near the mountain's summit. It was said that Pilate would appear in the nearby city of Lucerne and wreak his revenge should anyone be so foolish as to disturb him.

The city fathers of Lucerne put a strict ban on any attempt to scale Mt. Pilatus. Nevertheless, the six aforementioned clergymen went ahead with their climb, which was successful.

Their action did not arouse Pilate or any other demon. No disaster befell Lucerene. But when they returned, the clergymen were seized and imprisoned.

There were few attempts to climb tall mountains in the years that followed. Indeed, not until the 1850s, when English, French, and German climbers began to ascend the mid-European Alps, did mountaineering emerge as a sport. Superstitious beliefs do not die easily.

37

*I*t is an old custom in Greek households to bake a coin into a special cake, called the king's cake, or *basilopeta*, that is served on New Year's Day. The person who receives the piece of cake that contains the coin is to be blessed with good luck throughout the coming year.

The custom has always been followed in the home of Alex Campanis, a vice-president of the Los Angeles Dodgers. Campanis was born on Cos, one of the Dodecanese, a group of Greek islands in the Aegean Sea.

"The first piece of cake cut is set aside for the house," said Campanis. "The second piece is served to the master of the house, the next piece to the woman of the house, and then pieces go to the children and whatever relatives might be present."

Campanis has had good reason to believe in this piece of folklore. He received the lucky coin three times—in 1965, 1966, and 1974. In each one of those years, the Dodgers won the National League pennant.

*W*hen sprinter Carmen Brown went to the Olympic Games in Tokyo in 1964, she was given a pair of handsome red track shoes. They fit perfectly. They felt great. They became her lucky shoes.

In 1977, when she entered and won the 50-meter sprint in the Colgate Women's Games at Madison Square Garden, Carmen Brown was wearing the same shoes, now scuffed and battered and held together with strips of white adhesive tape. The spikes had been replaced several times.

"It happens all the time," said Fred Thompson, founder and coach of the Atoms Track Club of New York and the director of the Colgate Games. "An athlete gets fond of a certain pair of shoes, then starts believing they are good-luck shoes. They won't give them up, no matter what.

"Sometimes the shoes get so broken down that they can harm the athlete's performance. But they still keep them. I've known runners who have hidden their shoes from their coaches. They knew that if the coach got one look at them, they'd be made to wear a new pair.

"Of course, there's another side to the argument," Thompson continued. "To a great extent, success in track depends on one's mental attitude. If you believe that some object, such as a pair of lucky shoes, makes you perform better, then the object may, indeed, help."

Carmen Brown would certainly agree.

$\mathcal{P}$itcher Ron Bryant of the San Francisco Giants had been a major leaguer for two years, and most of it was a struggle. He managed to win only 5 of 13 decisions in 1970, only 7 of 17 the following year.

The 1972 season started just like the others, with Bryant losing more games than he won. He was beginning to await the moment that Giants manager Charlie Fox would tell him he was being shipped back to the minor leagues, where he had spent five dismal years. He shuddered at the thought.

Then one June day in Chicago, Bryant and catcher Dave Rader were leaving the hotel where the Giants were staying when Bryant saw a young girl holding a huge teddy bear. Bryant had always been called "Bear" by Mike Murphy, the Giants' equipment manager, and he decided to buy the bear and present it to Murphy as a joke.

The girl, who said she was a Cubs fan, wanted $30 for the bear. Bryant had only $25 with him. When Rader agreed to chip in $5, they were able to complete the transaction.

Bryant took the bear to the ballpark that afternoon, where he pitched a neat six-hitter, his best game in months. "Maybe it's the bear," he said to a teammate. "It brought me good luck."

Bryant began taking the bear with him everywhere. He plopped it into the seat next to him on the team bus. He perched it on a stool near his locker when he dressed for games. He sat it in the dugout when games were in progress, having garbed the bear in a Giants uniform shirt and cap.

Bryant became a consistent winner that year, winding up with 14 wins and 7 losses. The next year he made the bear his constant companion again. Whenever he was confronted with a tight situation during a game, Bryant would step off the rubber, then stare over at the bear, seemingly gaining strength from it. That year Bryant won 24 games. No other pitcher in the league won as many as 20.

"*Bear*-down Bryant," he came to be called. Some people said he was even beginning to have a facial resemblance to the bear.

Injuries plagued Bryant in 1974, and he had a sorry season, winning only 3 games. He was dealt to the St. Louis Cardinals in 1975, his final season as a major leaguer. He lost his only decision that year.

Now in retirement in Redlands, California, Bryant looks back with pleasure upon the two glittering seasons he had as major league pitcher. Some people say that the several fine young sluggers that the Giants were able to assemble in 1972 and 1973 were as much responsible for Bryant's victories as anything Bryant himself did.

Other people say that Bryant simply matured as a pitcher. He learned where to throw; he learned to change speeds.

Ask Bryant himself and he grins. "You can't give all the credit to the bear. There were several things involved," he's said. "But the bear sure had something to do with it."

When Joe Namath tempted fate in 1969 by predicting a Super Bowl victory for the New York Jets, everyone figured that Namath had no regard for the supernatural. Such wasn't the case. Namath did have a superstition of his own. He always made sure that his shoes were laced in a certain way.

"I lace them right over left," Namath once said. "I started doing that when I was working for the city of Beaver Falls [Pennsylvania], taking care of parks. A guy I was working with used to do it all the time."

Namath explained that he continued the practice because "life has been good, and why change it now?"

Namath would even switch the laces around if they weren't right over left, when he was given a new pair of shoes.

A half a century ago, Glenna Collett was the queen of women's golf. She won the U.S. Amateur championship four times—in 1922 and for three consecutive years beginning in 1928.

As she added to her championship string, she began to acquire a collection of trinkets and good-luck charms that she carried about with her on the course. It was said that she became so burdened down with small ornaments that she could have used an extra caddy just to carry them. And she got so that she performed so many rituals before taking a shot that it began to affect her ability to concentrate.

One day, Miss Collett lost an important match, nearly ran over a friend with her car, and then wrecked it. She immediately junked the whole lot of trinkets and abandoned superstitious practices for all time.

Among bowlers, both "name" bowlers and those of no more than average skills, the most common superstition is the custom of not filling in one's score as long as a string of strikes continues unbroken. Except for the strike symbol itself, frame after frame is left blank.

Bowlers are also superstitious about splits. (A split is a spare in which there is at least one pin down between the standing pins.) If a split occurs and is not converted into a spare, any bowler worth his salt will mark a heavy vertical line after that frame. The line—a "fence"—is meant to prevent that split from occurring again during the game.

Have you ever seen a split standing on a lane adjacent to the one on which you're bowling? A superstitious bowler would never think of rolling until that split has been cleared off.

Any conversation concerning superstitious tennis players eventually gets around to Art Larsen, winner of the U.S. Open at Forest Hills in 1950. If the official record manual had the category "Most Superstitions, Individual Player," Larsen would head the list, and no one would be close to him.

Larsen's superstitious practices developed out of a serious nervous condition he had that, in turn, resulted from combat duty he experienced in Europe during World War II. Larsen landed in Normandy not long after D-Day in 1944. Most members of his squadron were killed, some in a tragic strafing when U.S. Air Force planes mistook his unit for the enemy. But Larsen escaped without a scratch.

"I figured I'd done something lucky that day," Larsen was to explain years later. "Some good omen was watching out for me. I remembered I'd changed my socks, putting on my left one first, and I had eaten breakfast at a certain hour. The next day I followed the same routine, and the next, and the next." As his unit fought its way through France, Belgium, and into Luxembourg, Larsen stuck to his superstitious practices.

"By the time I got out of the Army and home to California, I had cultivated a whole string of superstitions and jinxes," Larsen recalled. "I had so many I couldn't count them."

Combat duty had left Larsen a bundle of nerves. He was too nervous to hold a job. Since he had once been a fine tennis player, doctors recommended that he take up the game again. The open-air exercise would help him, they advised.

"Tennis did me a lot of good, but I brought along a lot of jinxes," Larsen said. "You name 'em, I had 'em. I wouldn't let myself step on any kind of chalk line. Even in competition, I'd avoid the base line.

"I'd always tap the base line before serving, and I'd stand for a second with my back to the court. When I won a point, I'd always put the same ball back in play."

When Larsen awakened each morning, he received, he said, a "message" that told him what his lucky number was going to be for the day. It could be any number from 1 to 9.

Once he was informed of the number, Larsen would tap that number of times on the main objects he came in contact with. If the number happened to be 6, he'd tap six times. He'd tap with his hand, his foot, his tennis racket, or even with his head.

Larsen acquired an appropriate nickname, "Tappy."

Larsen was not only known for his multitude of superstitions, but for his stamina as well. He could play and play without tiring. In the year he won at Forest Hills, he seldom even bothered to sit down and rest when changing sides after the odd games, as players are entitled to do.

Larsen kept adding to his superstitious habits. Some were very peculiar. He once told a friend that a bird often perched on his shoulder during matches. Larsen would speak to the bird, revealing his private thoughts about the match. Since the bird was invisible, none of his opponents ever objected.

During the Wimbledon tournament one year, Larsen's bird caused him difficulty. A sparrow—a *real* sparrow—landed on the court during one of his matches. Larsen watched it for a few moments. Then suddenly he became upset, grabbed a ball, and hit it at the sparrow to frighten it away. The spectators, upset by Larsen's assault on a harmless sparrow, began to boo loudly. Larsen was forced to apologize.

Larsen later explained his conduct to a friend. "I thought," he said, "that the sparrow was going to attack *my* bird."

45

*J*ackie Charlton of Leeds United, one of England's best-known soccer teams, preferred to be the last player to leave the locker room when the players went out onto the field. His belief is said to have prevented him from becoming the team's captain. He then would have had to *lead* the team out.

*D*uring 1975, Obare Asiko, commissioner of the Kenya Football Federation, experienced a continuing problem with witch doctors. They were claiming that they could make the ball disappear or cast spells on opponents with bird and animal charms. Asiko called the practice "unsettling" and issued a warning to players, team officials, and fans that anyone found guilty of casting spells during soccer games would be subject to arrest and criminal prosecution.

Golfers are superstitious, too. For example, some golfers, when teeing off, will place the ball so that the trade name can be plainly seen.

Each dozen golf balls in a box is numbered from 1 to 12, so members of the same foursome can tell their balls apart. Naturally, there's a preference for certain numbers. Seven, of course, is the favorite.

Many golfers will not use a ball bearing any number above 4. They believe that doing so condemns them to a score of more than 4, usually par, on the hole they happen to be playing.

In his book *Superstition!* published in 1972, Willard Heaps reported on a study that involved 950 high school students. They were asked whether they believed that the sighting of a black cat meant that bad luck was going to follow. Forty percent of the students answered "yes" to the question, admitting they accepted the superstition to some degree.

The study was one of several that established the black cat as the basis for one of the three most commonly held superstitions of the present day. (Walking under a ladder and the number 13 are the two others.)

The superstition has been traced to the Middle Ages when it was believed that Satan sometimes took the form of a black cat when appearing before humans. The animal thus came to be the symbol of wickedness and misfortune.

Black cats have made several surprise appearances at sports events. The results are almost always noteworthy.

Take what happened in 1969 in baseball's National League. By midseason, it seemed the Chicago Cubs were on their way to the championship of the Eastern Division. Some people believed the New York Mets could challenge the Cubs. In mid-August, the Mets were in third place, nine games behind the Chicago team.

47

Then the Mets started winning and the Cubs began losing. The Cubs' lead had been cut to 2½ games when the team faced the Mets in a critical two-game series at Shea Stadium early in September.

The Mets took the first game, 3–2. The Cubs desperately needed to win the second game if they hoped to stifle the Mets' threat. Tom Seaver was to pitch for the New York team, Ferguson Jenkins for the Chicagoans.

In the first inning, as the Cubs' Glenn Beckert waited in the on-deck circle for his turn at bat, a black cat emerged from the runway behind home plate. The cat crossed behind Beckert and walked calmly toward the Cubs' dugout. When it reached the dugout, the cat stopped and peered in, studying the players.

"They put him out there," Ferguson Jenkins was to say after the game. But Jenkins never explained who "they" was.

The hex the cat produced became obvious in the third inning. Cleon Jones had singled for the Mets, and was forced at second by Art Shamsky. When Shamsky tried to steal, he got caught in a rundown, but he managed to make it into second safely when, yes, Glenn Beckert dropped the ball. Donn Clendenon followed with a home run, and the Cubs were down, 4–0.

The Chicago team went on to lose by a 7–1 score, a defeat that reduced their lead to a mere two percentage points and caused them to fall a game behind in the all-important "loss" column.

The Cubs were in low spirits, the players hardly speaking, as they left New York for a series in Philadelphia. There the team continued to sink. Within a week, the Cubs had totally collapsed, and they ended up in second place, a full eight games behind the Mets. The black-cat jinx had gone the limit.

No one knows for certain whether the Mets "planted" the black cat before that critical game against the Cubs. It is generally believed that they did not, that the cat was one of four or five that lived at Shea Stadium for the purpose of controlling the rat population. It just happened to appear when needed.

A planned appearance of a black cat took place several years later, in 1976, and involved Muhammad Ali, the great boxer. Not long before his fight with Ken Norton at Yankee Stadium, Ali learned that Norton had a fear of black cats. Ali plotted to make use of this information.

When it came time for the pre-fight medical examination, Ali asked that it be held at Norton's training camp instead of his own. Boxing observers were surprised. Why would Ali want to go to his opponent's camp? What was he planning?

On the day of the examination, Ali arrived at Norton's camp accompanied by a dozen of his friends, including Dick Sadler, one of his trainers. Sadler carried a little black box.

When Norton made his appearance, Sadler opened the box and a black cat jumped out. Norton's eyes grew wide and his mouth hung open. Ali watched and grinned. He knew that he had gained an advantage.

The fight lasted the full 15 rounds. Many fans thought Norton had won, but Ali was awarded a very close decision. Both judges gave 8 rounds to Ali, 7 to Norton. The referee scored it 8 rounds for Ali, 6 for Norton, and 1 even. Perhaps it was the black cat that provided Ali with the winning edge.

While the black cat is always associated with bad luck in this country, in England it's different. There the black cat means good luck.

The famed old Haymarket Theatre in London once had a pet black cat "to put the actors in good humor." In Yorkshire, in northeastern England, it was believed that a black cat in the house of a fisherman would ensure the safety of the husband at sea. Thieves used to kidnap black cats and sell them to fishermen's wives.

It is not surprising, then, that Virginia Wade, the graceful English tennis star who won the Wimbledon singles title in 1977, has always believed in the good fortune of black cats.

And she has a story to support her belief. Once, several years ago, on the night before an important match against Margaret Court, a black cat scurried across Virginia's path. She was elated. The next day she beat Margaret easily.

The British press, in hailing Virginia for her victory, praised her for her scorching serve and court quickness. But Virginia knew the real reason.

Many jockeys carry good-luck charms when they ride. They consider it bad luck to have their boots touch the floor before a race. They're kept on a shelf until the jockey is ready to don them. Dropping one's whip while mounting is also considered bad luck.

Trainers dislike having their horses photographed before a race. Whistling in the stable area is also looked upon with disfavor.

Harness racing is not without superstitions of its own. One says that it's bad luck to train horses on Sunday. Another stresses that a driver should never carry a black whip.

At all race tracks, the number 13 is carefully avoided. There are never any stalls in the stable area with the number 13. No horse carries that number on its saddlecloth in a race. Instead, the number 12A is substituted.

Even baseball fans indulge in a superstitious practice—the seventh-inning stretch. Hometown fans, without fail, stand at the end of the first half of the seventh inning to bring their team good luck. In some parks, the failure to rise can cause a person to be snubbed or even hooted at.

The custom of the seventh-inning stretch goes back to the days when pine planks without backs were used as seats. Sit on a plank for a while and cramped back muscles are sure to be a result. Stretching the muscles was a necessity, and the fans usually began standing and flexing around the sixth or seventh inning. It wasn't long before the fans settled on the seventh inning itself, 7 being regarded as a lucky number.

The seventh-inning stretch isn't the only superstition that fans have. Some will enter the stadium only through what they believe to be a lucky gate. "Every time I go through this gate, the Yankees win," a fan told a ticket-taker at Yankee Stadium not long ago.

But another fan passed by the ticket-taker. "Your gate's a jinx," she told him.

Once in a while a fan will refuse to take the rain check. "Keep it!" a fan told a ticket-taker. "It's bad luck!"

In two decades as an outstanding performer in women's softball, fireballing Joan Joyce struck out 6,171 batters, pitched 110 no-hitters, and 35 perfect games. In eighteen of those twenty years, she was an All-Star selection.

In a twelve-year span that ended in 1975, she led her team, the Raybestos Brakettes, to ten Amateur Softball Association championships. In 1976 she joined the Connecticut Falcons of the International Women's Professional Softball Association.

Joan overwhelmed batters with her searing fastball, which was once timed at 116 miles an hour. Even Nolan Ryan of the California Angels, considered the fastest of baseball's fastballers, has not been as fast as Joan.

With her kind of speed, Joan hardly had need for outside assistance. But once in her career, she was helped by a superstition.

It was in 1968. The Brakettes were competing in the A.S.A. championship play-offs.

"After we had won an important game, we decided we wouldn't change uniforms until we had won the title," Joan recalled. The players' red and white jerseys and pin-striped satin shorts quickly became smudged with dirt and stained with sweat. The tournament went on and on, the Brakettes finally winning.

Joan has had mixed feelings about what it took to win. "Those uniforms, my God, they were awful," she's said with a shudder. "I could never go through that again."

*D*uring the 1935 baseball season, the Chicago Cubs swept twenty-one games in a row on their way to winning the National League pennant. Only one other time in baseball history has a team managed to win as many as twenty-one consecutive games.

As victory piled on victory, the Cubs became more and more superstitious. The players would not let the laundryman take away their uniforms for cleaning. Phil Wrigley, the team's owner, lit a cigarette every time the team went to bat, and he kept it burning for as long as the team continued its turn at the plate.

On the day the winning streak started, a twelve-year-old boy, a friend of the son of one of the players, happened to sit on the bench. The Cubs convinced him to stay on the bench as long as they kept winning. He didn't run errands. He didn't serve as a batboy. He just sat.

*A*nother well-known baseball superstition is to avoid the use of the term "no-hitter" when a pitcher is working on one. Many years ago a broadcaster named Red Barber defied this tradition—and saw the fates respond.

The occasion was the fourth game of the 1947 World Series, the Brooklyn Dodgers vs. the New York Yankees. Yankee pitcher Bill Bevens was one out away from the first no-hitter in World Series history. Barber felt he owed it to his radio audience to tell them the complete story. Hardly was the phrase "no-hitter" out of his mouth, when the Dodgers' Cookie Lavagetto smacked a double that not only ended Bevens' chance for lasting fame, but provided the tying and winning runs. In the weeks that followed, Yankee fans bombarded Barber with angry letters.

When the Yankees' Don Larsen hurled his perfect game in the 1956 World Series, not allowing a single batter to reach first base, announcers were more cautious. After the seventh inning, one remarked that the Yankees had "twenty-one straight putouts." Another noted that "no Dodger has reached first base." They were careful to avoid the terms "no-hitter" and "perfect game" until the feat was actually accomplished.

New York City newspaperman Joe Williams recalled being in the press box at Yankee Stadium during the game Larsen pitched. "Along about the seventh inning," Williams said, "I happened to remark, 'You know, this guy could be on his way to the first perfect game ever pitched in the World Series.'

"My press-box neighbors froze in horror," said Williams. "You'd have thought I vandalized a sacred painting or slurred the flag."

The next perfect game occurred on June 21, 1964. Jim Bunning of the Philadelphia Phillies was the pitcher. The New York Mets were the victims.

"I mentioned 'no-hitter' and 'perfect game,' and I counted the outs," Bunning once recalled. "Why not? The thing was no secret. It was out there on the scoreboard for everyone to see. And, besides, talking about it helped to break the tension."

Bunning's attitude must be considered the exception, however. On May 8, 1968, Jim (Catfish) Hunter, a member of the Oakland A's at the time, pitched a perfect game against the Minnesota Twins, only the ninth perfect game in major league history. "I didn't realize that I had a perfect game going at the time," Hunter recalled. "I thought it was only a no-hitter. But I didn't say anything about it. And no one else in the dugout did, either."

As baseball entered the decade of the 1970s, the superstition was still being carefully observed. Bill White, who played for the St. Louis Cards and Philadelphia Phils during the 1960s, and later became a broadcaster for the New York Yankees, recently told how he feels about the practice. "If a no-hitter is being pitched, I do inform the people," said White. "When I give the score at the end of an inning, I'll say, for example, 'For the Yankees, six runs on eight hits; for the Indians, no runs and no hits.'

"But I avoid using the term 'no-hitter.' I try not to make a big thing out of it."

55

Fans of the Dallas Cowboys used to believe that wide receiver Golden Richards was a sloppy dresser because his right sock was always lower than his left. It wasn't that Richards was careless, however. He believed that he *had* to wear his socks that way, and that if he failed to do so he might never catch a touchdown pass again.

very athlete is familiar with the word "whammy," which refers to a supernatural spell cast over an opponent that helps to subdue him. The Pittsburgh Pirates used to have their own whammy artist in catcher Earl Smith, who played for the team from 1924 until 1928.

Smith would trigger the whammy by waving his mitt in the batter's face as he stepped into the batter's box. One or two waves of the glove was usually sufficient, although a particularly dangerous hitter would be given an extra dose.

Once this was done, the hitter was supposedly rendered quite helpless. If he did happen to get a hit, Smith dismissed it as an accident.

Smith had begun his career with the New York Giants in 1919. But after an argument with Giants manager John McGraw, he was traded away. Smith took particular delight in beating the Giants and exercising the whammy on his former teammates.

The most memorable display of Smith's talents took place during the 1925 World Series. The Pirates faced the Washington Senators. Smith concentrated his efforts on Leon (Goose) Goslin, a fearsome hitter who could knock a baseball out of shape, and frequently did. He led the American League in home runs that season. Every time Goslin stepped up to the plate, Smith performed his bizarre routine.

Of course, no one knows for sure how much Smith's antics rattled Goslin and the other Washington hitters. But a couple of facts are clear: the Pirates, who weren't given much of a chance against the powerful Senators, managed to win the Series, with Pittsburgh's Red Oldham striking out the final batter in the seventh game. And the man who fanned was Goose Goslin.

Many superstitious beliefs have been associated with the horse. A spotted horse or one with patches of color was believed to have magical gifts. A hair from such an animal was recommended in the treatment of certain illnesses.

Horses were thought to be quite helpless in defending themselves against the evil eye and its effects. To protect their animals, owners fastened small bells or brass disks to their harnesses. Another method of warding off harm was to attach a small piece of red cloth to the horse's forehead.

The good luck and other special qualities assigned to the horseshoe have little to do with the horse. They're often traced to a legend involving the devil and a blacksmith named Dunstan. One day the devil came to Dunstan to have a hoof reshod. Dunstan, recognizing his visitor, seized him, bound him, and began to torture him. Dunstan released his prisoner only when the devil promised that neither he nor his helpers would ever enter a building protected by a horseshoe.

When hanging a horseshoe, you must remember to put the open end up. Put the open end down, and the horseshoe's luck will run out.

Tennis star Ray Moore, who was born in Johannesburg, South Africa, believes that green is his lucky color. But such wasn't always the case.

"I had a green outfit that I lost in for something like four consecutive weeks," Moore explained. "Then one day I happened to be matched against an opponent that I thought I could beat easily. I decided to wear the green outfit again, just to break the pattern.

"Well, I lost.

"I put the outfit away and decided not to wear it again until I was in a big match and I was expected to lose.

"Well, I wore it in a big match, and I won. I tried it again, and I won again. I did it four more times—and each time I won.

"Now my green outfit is my lucky outfit. I even wear it when I'm the underdog." Not long after Moore told this story, he defeated Bjorn Borg, the world's top-seeded player at the time, in the U.S. Pro Indoor Championships. And Moore was wearing the green outfit.

*D*uring the 1975–1976 hockey season, Red Kelly, coach of the Toronto Maple Leafs, became a believer in pyramid power. He swore there was a great source of strength not only in pyramid-shaped structures themselves, but even in drawings of them. Kelly lined the underside of the Toronto bench with pyramid illustrations.

Center Darryl Sittler, the captain of the Leafs at the time, was asked what he thought of Kelly's theory.

"Pyramids?" said Sittler, his brow wrinkling. "I don't buy that stuff. After all, how many hockey teams are there in Egypt?"

*H*ockey players are well known for their superstitious practices, and the Philadelphia Flyers, winners of the Stanley Cup in 1974 and again in 1975, had more superstitious quirks than most teams. For example, when the Flyers came out onto the ice before each period, Gary Dornhoefer always had to be the last player to leave the locker room. Don Saleski had to be the next to last.

As the team began its warm-ups and defenseman André (Moose) Dupont skated by the starting goaltender, he tapped him with his stick and demanded that the goalie tap him back. If the goalie happened to forget, Dupont would circle back and go into a holding position in front of the goal until the goalie tapped him.

Dupont was very serious about this. He was known to scream at any goalie who failed to keep up his part of the ritual.

Fred Stolle, coach of the New York Apples of World Team Tennis, has always sat on the same spot on the bench to bring his team good luck. "No one else would think of sitting there," Billie Jean King, a member of the Apples, has said. "That spot is Fred's, and Fred's alone."

Around the race track, nobody likes gray horses. Even worse are horses with four white feet. Any prospective buyer who is the least bit familiar with thoroughbreds is aware of this age-old advice:

> One white foot, go ahead and buy him;
>   Two white feet, you'd better try him;
> Three white feet, look well about him;
>   Four white feet, you'd best do without him.

The Washington Redskins' George Allen has been one of the most superstitious of all football coaches. The number 13 never failed to make him nervous.

One afternoon after a practice before an important game against the Colts, Allen addressed his players. "We have all of Baltimore's games on film," he said. "You can borrow some films, and check out a projector and take it home with you."

Then he turned to an assistant. "We have plenty of projectors, don't we?"

"We sure do," said the assistant. "We have thirteen of them."

Allen scowled. "Did you say thirteen?"

"Yes, I did."

"First thing tomorrow," Allen instructed, "either go out and buy another projector, or break one."

Anxiety over the number 13 is widespread in the sports world. Some athletes merely avoid the number, while others actually fear it. But virtually everyone acknowledges the number's special meaning in some way.

Athletes have shown their respect for number 13 in many different ways. It used to be common knowledge that there were thirteen steps in the flight of stairs that led from the visiting club's dressing room to the dugout runway at Fenway Park in Boston. Countless players hopped over the last step to avoid the 13 hoodoo.

Several years ago, when Leo Durocher was managing the Chicago Cubs, he demonstrated his belief in the number 13 hex. When his team arrived in Montreal for a series with the Expos, his players were assigned to the thirteenth floor of the Queen Elizabeth Hotel. Durocher himself drew Room 1313. As soon as the Cubs lost a game, Durocher told newspaper reporters that the room assignments had jinxed his players.

The spell cast by the number affects tennis players, too. Andy Pattison did things in multiples of 4 during a match. He'd sometimes count off his steps in fours. He would bounce a ball four times or eight times before a serve.

"But I never bounce the ball or do anything else twelve times," said

Pattison. "The next time would be the thirteenth time. I don't do anything on the number 13."

There have always been exceptions, individual athletes who violated common practice and flaunted the number 13 on their uniforms. One was running back Kenny Washington, who starred for UCLA in the late 1940s and later for the Los Angeles Rams. Washington had such success wearing the number 13 as a college player that the Bruins retired his jersey to the trophy case.

Ralph Branca, who played for the Brooklyn Dodgers, wore the number 13 and became well known for it. Branca was a mainstay of the Brooklyn pitching staff during the late 1940s. A tall right-hander, he boasted a splendid 21–12 record in 1947.

Branca believed that the number 13 had special significance for him. There were seven boys and six girls in his family, which, as he liked to point out, added up to 13. He wore a size 13 shoe. The digits of his home telephone number totaled 13. It was fitting, Branca thought, to wear uniform number 13.

Everything went fine until 1951, when Branca had to struggle to win as many games as he lost. But the Dodgers had other pitchers to take up the slack, and by early August had a stranglehold on the rest of the league, leading by 13½ games. Then the New York Giants began to move. Week by week they chipped away at the Dodgers' lead, and on the day the season ended the two teams were in a flat-footed tie.

A three-game play-off was ordered. The Giants won the first game. The Dodgers won the second game, then took a commanding 4–1 lead into the ninth inning of the final contest.

When the Giants batted in the last of the ninth, Whitey Lockman doubled following a pair of singles. One run scored, narrowing the Dodger advantage to two runs. Runners were on second and third.

It was Bobby Thomson's turn to bat. But before Thomson stepped up, Dodger manager Chuck Dressen went to the mound to tell Don Newcombe that he was through for the day. Dressen then summoned Branca in from the bullpen.

Branca's first pitch was a called strike. Branca checked the base runners and delivered again. Thomson swung hard and slammed the ball high and far. Branca turned to watch its flight. It landed in the left-field stands—a home run.

As Thomson danced around the bases, and the joyous Giants fans whooped and hollered, Branca, tears welling up in his eyes, walked slowly from the mound.

The next year when Branca appeared at spring training, he was wearing number 12. The Dodger management, he explained, had forced him to give up his ill-omened number 13. "They told me they'd fine me if I ever wore it again," he said.

64

British golfers are said to be much more superstitious than their American counterparts. This is partly because they have been playing the game about two hundred years longer than Americans, and thus have had more time to develop superstitious habits.

One well-known British custom is expressed by the saying, "Two up and five to play never won a match." This means that when a golfer is leading an opponent by two strokes with five holes remaining, he will wind up losing the match.

The superstition is said to have originated in Scotland in the 1700s. On several occasions, players who were two strokes ahead with five holes to play, played poorly and lost.

Actually, this is another "unlucky 13" superstition. The golfer in question, since he had five holes to play, had just completed the thirteenth hole.

Boxers often have lucky charms sewn into their trunks. Joe Gans, who won the lightweight championship in 1902, always carried a pair of his favorite dice into the ring. Jack Johnson, the heavyweight champion for seven years beginning in 1908, always tucked a ten-dollar bill into his trunks before entering the ring. Another heavyweight champion, Jersey Joe Walcott, relied on a rabbit's foot.

Billie Jean King's many achievements as a tennis star won her recognition as Woman Athlete of the Year in 1967 and again in 1973. It would take a page at least this size to list all of the tennis titles that Billie Jean has won.

Of all of the tournaments in which Billie Jean competed, Wimbledon was her favorite. "Everything is first class," she once said. "To me, it's the Number 1 tournament in the world. Just stepping out on the court there is a thrill."

Her attitude toward the tournament may help to explain Billie Jean's success there. Her stunning victory over Evonne Goolagong in 1975 was Billie Jean's sixth singles title at Wimbledon, and her nineteenth title overall. In all of Wimbledon history, only one other player has won as many as nineteen titles.

Billie Jean was once called the "queen of mannerisms." She has performed little tap steps or run her fingers through her hair when she was on the court. When angered by an official's call, she's raised a clenched fist toward the heavens.

Some of her mannerisms were unconscious, while others were deliberate. None of her mannerisms, however, had its root in any superstitious belief.

But Billie Jean did admit to having one superstitious practice to which she was devoted. And it involved Wimbledon. "Whenever I go to Wimbledon," she once said, "I always make sure I use the same bathtub."

eo Durocher, a major league manager for more than two decades up until the early 1970s, was often said to lead both leagues in superstitions. His desk in the clubhouse was always cluttered with good-luck charms sent to him by fans, and he had countless superstitious practices that he followed.

One became his trademark. When his team came to bat and Durocher went out to coach at third base, he would walk to the bag and tap it with his foot three times. He would then use his cleats to rub out the white chalk lines that formed the coach's box.

Once, when Durocher was manager of the New York Giants, the team visited Ebbets Field for a series with their hometown rivals, the Brooklyn Dodgers. The Dodger ground crew sought to unsettle Durocher by digging the lines of the coaching box to a depth of six inches, and then filling in the narrow trench with white clay. Durocher would never erase *that* line, the ground crew assumed.

But Durocher proved equal to the challenge. Once he figured out what the ground crew had done, he simply kicked enough dirt over the line to cover it up.

aseball players aren't the only ones to steer clear of field markings. Vitas Gerulaitis, one of tennis' most colorful performers, has never permitted himself to step on a court line before a match. Betty Stove, a member of the Sea-Port Cascades and one of the leading players in World Team Tennis, has had the same superstition. "Betty would rather break an ankle than step on a line," said her frequent doubles partner, Billie Jean King.

Some women's sports stars wear lucky clothes when they compete. With others, it's lucky jewelry. But Billie Billing, a top-ranking pool player, puts her faith in an entirely different object. Whenever Billie chalks her cue, as a player must do before each shot, she does it with a cube of lucky chalk.

Throughout most of her career, Billie has struggled to defeat the amazing Jean Balukas, the Brooklyn, New York, teenager who won her sixth consecutive U.S. Open Pocket Billiards Championship in 1977. But Billie never has. In February 1977, Billie lost again to her long-time rival, but this time the score was close, 100–87.

Afterward, Billie picked up the piece of blue chalk she had used and carefully tucked it away in her cue case. She's used the chalk in every match since and plans to continue using it. Billie finished fourth in the U.S. Open in 1977, but she's hoping that one day soon the lucky chalk will help her to defeat Jean Balukas and carry her to the title.

Ann Carr's career as a gymnast hit a high point in 1977 when, as a nineteen-year-old freshman at Penn State, she won the all-around title at the A.I.A.W. (Association for Intercollegiate Athletics for Women) National Gymnastics Championships.

Did a superstition help?

"When I was eleven or twelve and first began to compete, I had all kinds of superstitions," she recalls. "I'd make it a point to always wear the same gym shoes, and I'd carry the same gym bag. Or I'd have a lucky hair ribbon, and I'd wear it in meet after meet after meet, no matter how wrinkled it became."

But as her career unfolded, Ann's attitude toward her superstitious practices began to change. Following an injury in 1975, she staged a dramatic comeback to win five gold medals in the Pan American Games. She suffered another setback in 1976 when she sprained her ankle, an injury that kept her sidelined for the Olympic Games. But not long after, she scored her triumph in the A.I.A.W. Nationals.

"All the ups and downs I had made me think differently about my superstitions," she says. "I realized that the hair ribbon I happened to be wearing or the gym bag I was carrying weren't responsible for all the things that were happening to me."

One by one, Ann began to discard her superstitious habits. At the time she won the A.I.A.W. title in 1977, she was superstition-free.

Crossed bats used to be regarded as a bad-luck sign by baseball players, and some would cringe at the sight of them. Some players still do.

Julio Gotay, a second baseman for the Houston Astros during the late 1960s, refused to play near the bag one inning. His manager shouted at him from the dugout, trying to get him to move. But Gotay refused to change his position.

The mystified manager finally stopped the game and went out to see what was wrong. There were crossed bats in front of the dugout, explained Gotay, and if he moved closer to second base he would be able to see them. The bats were uncrossed, and Gotay then moved to where the manager wanted him.

Later in the game, the manager was ejected for arguing with the umpire. Gotay blamed it on the hex produced by the crossed bats.

Index